INNER G: HOW TO MANIFEST SUCCESS IN YOUR LIFE

ERIC BELL

COVER DESIGN BY MARIAH EVANS

COPYRIGHT ©2019 BY ERIC BELL. ALL RIGHTS RESERVED. PRINTED IN THE UNITED STATES OF AMERICA. NO PART OF THIS PUBLICATION MAY BE REPRODUCED OR DISTRIBUTED IN ANY FORM OR BY ANY MEANS, OR STORED IN A DATABASE OR RETRIEVAL SYSTEM, WITHOUT THE PRIOR WRITTEN PERMISSION OF THE PUBLISHER.

ALLMIGHTY PUBLISHING

ISBN 978-0-9996621-2-0

INTRODUCTION

They say that insanity is when you do the same thing and expect different results. If you want to see positive changes in your life, and you feel as if you are not where you should be at this point in your life, then it is time for you to start doing things differently. It's just as simple, yet complex to some as this. Your position in life right now is the sum product of your daily habits. These daily habits that you have adopted over the years have helped shaped how you view yourself. In order to get the ball rolling in the right direction it is time for you to change the way that you view yourself, and it is time to adopt better habits. Basically, it is time for you to become the change that you want to see in yourself.

    My purpose for writing this book is simple. I notice a lot of people are not satisfied in life. Just observe, and you will see that a large majority of the population are just unhappy. Some people do a good job of concealing this unhappiness, while others cannot mask the pain. Depression is real, and it cannot be ignored. I simply decided to write this book to inform you that you don't have to seek for external resources to gain control of your life. The power that you seek lies right within you; you just have to activate it. You don't need outside permission to be great. You don't need outside permission to be happy and at peace. My goal for the readers of this book is that after you read this you will begin the journey of adopting more positive habits, and you become more productive in your daily life, which will help you construct the life you deserve.

It's time to come to grips with the actual reality, and get out of la la land. If you want to become a better person in life, you have to begin by doing better things in life. You want to become a more productive person in life; you have to start doing more productive things in life. No way around this. You can't just wish, hope, and pray for change without being willing to put in the work required for the change to happen. It is time you exercise the true inner power that you possess. You are searching for the gold on the outside, but the MOST VALUABLE GOLD, is right there within you. You are a true source of wealth, happiness, health, and peace, once you simply activate that energy within you, everything will form accordingly. It's time to give yourself permission to be GREAT, TODAY!

1. *YOU SPEAK TO THE UNIVERSE*

There is this common belief amongst people that revolves around the Universe providing them with signs. Some will also substitute God/Energy, or whatever they may believe for the Universe. If this is you then cool, but I am asking you to open your mind for a moment. I am asking you to open up to a new perspective that may make a ton of sense once you really begin to think about it.

One of the biggest reasons why I see a lot of people fail to manifest the lives that they deserve is that they have a lack of confidence, or they sit around and wait for opportunities and signs. In this day and age, you will not get too far sitting around waiting for someone to give you a chance, or waiting around for the perfect circumstances. Good things don't come to those who wait; good things come to those who create.

I am pretty sure you have been around people, or have heard people speak about how the universe has given them a sign. Some people even like to wait for the Universe to speak to them so that they can attain some much needed guidance and direction. What if I told you that what you seek from the Universe, you possess within, and you have the power to speak to the Universe?

That's right, you don't have to wait around for the Universe to give you a sign, instead you speak what you WANT, NEED, and DESERVE into the Universe and see what happens. You don't need to wait for the Universe to tell you what path you are on, you tell the Universe where you are headed and the Universe will shape up according to YOUR thoughts, words, and actions. You possess the power; all you have to do is start exercising it.

What If I told you, the Universe is waiting for YOU to give it some direction and guidance? What happens is, the Universe reacts to your thoughts, that's why you even get those "signs" in the first place. Those are all manifestations based off of the power of one's mind. If you fail to speak to the Universe and let it know what you want and need to happen, then it will simply provide you with signs based off of the quality of your current thoughts, which for most people is relatively negative.

Your mind, both the conscious and subconscious mind are one with the Universe, and your subconscious mind never sleeps. It is always striving to act upon the impressions that you place upon it. The subconscious mind cannot differentiate between reality and fiction that is why it is very important to monitor the quality of your thoughts. If you want something to happen, think it, write it down, visualize it, speak it consistently and watch how the subconscious mind works to manifest whatever it is that you want to happen.

Instead of us exercising this mental power that we all possess, a lot of us tend to let external forces takeover, and influence our minds the most. We like to take on lives that other people feel as though we should take on. We like to take on the "American Dream" or lives of others that we may see on the television screen or online. Instead of being original, and authentic beings, we become victims of outside influence. Do not become a character in someone else's book, you have one life to leave a legacy behind, speak it into existence.

You may be wondering how exactly do you exercise this power. Well, to me it is rather simple; I like to use affirmations to let the Universe know what will happen. And when speaking these affirmations you have to speak it as if you've already accomplished whatever it is you are striving to accomplish in life. Then you must live as if you've already accomplished it as well.

If you have a goal to become wealthier, then start simple by simply repeating to yourself, "I am wealthy." Just start there and see how everything starts to change, drastically in your life. This is rather simple, and it will cause dramatic shifts in your life. Once you get the hang of this simple strategy, then you can go more in depth, and start creating more detailed, and specific affirmations revolving around whatever the goal that you have is.

Two other great affirmations, or mantras that I got out of a book goes a little something like this, "I like myself" and "Something good will happen to me today." Repeat these mantras throughout the day to yourself, and I am telling you, your confidence and self-esteem will sky rocket, and trust me something good will definitely happen to you. I have had people inform me of how they implemented this strategy, and on day one they had a positive experience.

One lady informed me, that the day she saw me mention this, she did it, and she just happened to win some money on that day. Don't underestimate the power of your thoughts and words.

The key when it comes to these affirmations are to use them to neutralize any negative thought that is trying to arise within your mind. As soon as you feel that negative thought creeping up, it is time to repeat your affirmation. You can also use it as a preventative measure, by repeating the affirmations as soon as you rise in the morning, and before you go to sleep at night. There's power in your words, remember that, everything starts with a thought; you become what you think about.

So, before we dive into the next section of this book, I want you to stop what you are doing right now and create your affirmation. It can be short and sweet like the I am wealthy mantra, or it can be as specific as telling yourself you doubled your income within the next six months. The time is NOW to create your affirmation, and commit to the mantra. Reading is just one part of the equation; you must implement the information that you consume to improve. Don't proceed any further until you have created your mantra, and repeat it to yourself at least three times before moving on. Speak to the Universe, let it know who and what you are, and how your life will unfold!

2. ***THE EARLY RISER***

In this section, I am going to provide you with a tool that I have just started implementing that has helped me tremendously in regards to gaining control over my life. How many of you would consider yourselves a morning person? Don't worry, if you were anything like I was about a month or two ago you would laugh at the thought of someone suggesting you start waking up about an hour or two earlier than you have to be up to get things done. Well, that is exactly what I am suggesting, because becoming an early riser has catapulted my life in the right direction.

First things first, I want to give credit to the Authors, Hal Elrod and David Osborn for their work in the book, *Miracle Morning Millionaires*. I suggest everyone get a copy of that book and read it twice. That book has been a key part for me in regards to turning my life around and getting more accomplished in my life. The first portion of this section will be a little personal just to show you all how far I've come, in the short time that I've been implementing this strategy.

MY MORNING MIRACLE STORY

I am 28 years old, and I graduated from college in 2013 with two degrees. Along with that, four years later I became a certified personal trainer. Everything sounds good, right? Wrong, I have been unable to locate a decent job since graduation, and it has been rather difficult for me to fully commit to personal training the way that I would like to because of bad financial decisions I made in the past due to the fact that I've had to work jobs that I KNOW are an insult to my true abilities. Does this sound like something you can relate to, or at least know someone who is suffering from this? I bet, because a lot of people in this country are going through this same struggle. We believed in the American Dream, only for it to be just that, a dream, not reality.

Well, instead of me sitting around waiting for opportunities, or praying and wishing for things to get better, I took a more productive approach. I thought to myself there has to be a better way. Spending eight to ten hours in these corporations just to STILL not make enough money to enjoy life is not the life I deserve. I was in this zone where I felt like something needed to change, because obviously what I was already doing was only making me more miserable by the day.

The first thing that hit me was the fact that I realized in order for things to turnaround, I had to find a way to be more productive with the time that I already have. This boiled down to two options for me, I could either start staying up later than usual, or I could start getting up earlier in the morning. Well, in my studies of the wealthy and successful, I found that they all had one thing in common they all were early risers. Once I came across this common trend, I decided that I would become an early riser too.

Well, in the beginning this was A LOT easier said than done. Throughout my life, I have never been what one would consider a morning person. I was what you would consider a night owl. When it came to waking up in the morning, I had a hard time getting up. It seemed like it never really mattered what time I went to sleep the night before either. Just the thought of getting up early in the morning had always been unattractive to me. But I knew this was something I had to start doing if I wanted to become more productive in my life.

In the beginning of trying to create this new habit, I failed, A LOT. I would get up, turn off the alarm, and go right back to sleep. I know this sounds way too familiar. I was a snooze champion. In which I came across a wonderful quote that deals with one continually hitting the snooze button. I am paraphrasing, but the quote went something along the lines of hitting the snooze button doesn't make much sense because it is basically stating that you don't like getting up in the morning so you repeat that process over and over again by hitting the snooze button.

In the beginning, I just couldn't seem to get it right. I would wake up one morning, but then the next few days I would pound the snooze button into the ground. I wrestled with this for a few months actually, and it was a long process to master this particular habit, but I am proud to say that now I am able to rise early and be productive with no problem.

You may be wondering what happened, what enabled me to finally break the bad habit and start rising early? Well, I came across a few valuable pieces of advice that assisted me on this journey. The first piece of advice was simple, something so simple that I was upset that I hadn't thought about it when I read about it. Simply placing my phone, which is my alarm out of reach, helped me tremendously. The simple act of getting out of the bed was a key piece that helped me overcome my morning struggles.

The next piece of advice that was helpful for me was when I was informed to set my intentions for the morning the night before. This simply means that before you go to sleep, you kind of reflect on what you will get accomplished in the upcoming morning. What this does is it helps you become more eager for the morning. This gives you a purpose for waking up in the morning.

If you are just waking up in the morning just to say you wake up early, then you will not be very successful when it comes to making this a habit. You have to have a purpose; you have to have a reason for waking up each and every morning. This is where you take the small steps necessary to reach the big goals you have set for yourself. Wake up with a purpose. Wake up with the intention of getting things done.

The last thing I will touch on when it comes to becoming an early riser is creating a ritual in the morning. This goes hand in hand with waking up with a purpose, and setting your intentions the night before. If you watch sports, then I am sure that you have seen players who have certain rituals before the game actually starts. Some of them may seem awkward, but performing these rituals before they perform helps them get into the right state of mind for the game. I also suggest you develop a routine, or ritual for the morning.

My recommendation is at the beginning, you slowly add on things to your morning ritual. First, you simply want to develop the habit of actually waking up in the morning. You don't want to start off by overwhelming yourself with an hour-long morning ritual that you may or may not perform. For instance, I started off by doing something that I KNEW I would do, which is reading. When I first started waking up in the morning, I would immediately grab a book and start reading. When developing a habit, you have to make it attractive in the beginning stages. So, since reading is something I love to do, the fact that I was able to get more reading done by waking up in the morning helped me develop the habit.

Once I was doing this for about two weeks, I felt that it was time to add another element or two to my morning routine. This is when I added the element of typing to the equation. This is how I was able to complete this book. It feels great to be able to get important work done early in the morning before most people get out of the bed.

Lastly, I would recommend that you add in elements to your morning ritual that helps your mind & body. What I mean by this is you should be looking to add elements like mediation, affirmations, stretching, light exercising, drinking water, and eating fruits to your morning routine. When you get a healthy start to the day, this will set you up for a very healthy and productive day.

I will provide you with an acronym that I got from the book, *Miracle Morning Millionaires* that helped me out tremendously. The acronym is **S.A.V.E.R.S** and it stands for Silence, Affirmations, Visualization, Exercise, Read, and Scribing. If you are having troubles with establishing a routine for your morning, then I suggest starting with this strategy.

OWN YOUR MORNING

I cannot stress the importance of owning your morning enough. If there is one thing that I know for sure that will help turn your life around it is this. This is something that you should implement, NOW. We have to stop making excuses and just start executing. We all have the same amount of time to get things done. Some people are just more effective with their time.

If that is the excuse you are going to roll with in regards to why you haven't accomplished a goal, then you need to sit down and do some serious reflecting. You DO have enough time to get some exercising in. You DO have enough time to get some reading done. You DO have enough time to meal prep so that you can lose the weight, and start eating healthier. Time is precious, and it should not be wasted. How are you using your time?

3. **_UNDERSTANDING SELF_**

How often have you sat down and faced your weaknesses? Like, how often have you really sat down and had an honest conversation with yourself about areas where you can improve in life? A lot of us fail to make strides in the right direction because we are afraid to face our own weaknesses and fears. You will not grow if you are afraid to critique your own self.

Too often we sit around and wait for others to tell us the truth about ourselves. You've seen this too often. You know how you'll have a few people point out the obvious to you, and then you begin to think that maybe, just maybe these people are right about you. Say that you have trouble listening to other people. Deep down you know you don't listen, but you never really sit down with SELF and get to the bottom of this bad trait, instead you try to ignore it. Instead, you leave it up to other people to have to repeatedly tell you that you do not listen.

What will happen the first few times you are told this? You will be in that state of denial. You will deny the truth in it at first because you've been neglecting SELF. You will immediately place the blame on the other people. You are not the one, who doesn't listen, people don't listen to you. You make yourself out to be the victim here, everyone is just picking, or hating on you. The sad thing is, some people actually stay in this state of denial and become stuck in their ways. This is why self-reflection should be a consistent routine for people.

If you cannot be honest with yourself, then what are you even living for? You should be the best knower of self, not anyone else. In order for us to grow we have to be able to KNOW and UNDERSTAND who we are as individuals. You have to be able to identify your strengths and weaknesses. A lot of people have no problem identifying their strengths (and this is even debatable), but when it comes to our weaknesses, we definitely do not want to face reality.

You are doing yourself a big disservice by not getting in tune with yourself. Knowledge of self is very important. If you fail to understand what makes you happy, and what makes you unhappy, then you will have a hard time creating the life that you deserve. You have to know what type of environments you thrive in, and vice versa. You have to know and understand what type of people you work best with, and vice versa. This will help you figure out what type of career path to travel down, and which paths to avoid. Honestly, a lot of us are living in misery because we are forcing ourselves to be in environments that are not conducive to our personalities.

This is what I need for you to start doing immediately. I need for you to begin to pay close attention to yourself. Pay attention to the small details in your life, and take notes. Keep a journal with you, and jot down every noticeable detail whether it is a sign from a dream, or an interaction you had with a stranger. Take notes of the things that make you feel negative, and note why it makes you feel that way. If you don't know why something makes you feel a certain type of way immediately, then ponder on it until you come up with some reasons. Stop leaving it up to outsiders to diagnose you and tell you what your problems are. I get it, sometimes that outside evaluation is necessary and helpful, but most of the time WE KNOW the problems and the solutions we just tend to ignore them.

I want you to spend some time getting to KNOW YOURSELF. When someone asks you the question, "Who are you?" You should be able to answer this question promptly with confidence. And when you get acquainted with yourself, then it's time to place yourself in environments that reflect the person you are. If you are currently in an environment that is not conducive to your health and well-being, then remove yourself from such environment. Most people in this country are unhappy, especially when it comes to the jobs that we work. How great would it be to do something that you love and makes you happy, all the while being able to provide for your family, AND then some?

We have to stop compromising our happiness. Once you figure out what really makes you unhappy, then it is time to focus on your strengths. Once you know and understand what you DO NOT want to do, then it's time to focus on what it is that you WANT TO DO. You have one life to live, why not spend it being happy and doing something you enjoy doing? You deserve to be happy and at peace, do not let anyone tell you otherwise.

4. *BE BOLD, BE COURAGEOUS, BE AUTHENTIC*

The world that we live in has conditioned us to live in fear. What kind of fear am I talking about? The fears that I am referring to are being yourself and taking risks. We have been conditioned to accept the "American dream" and strive to live comfortably. Well, the only way to truly elevate in life is to get out of your comfort zone and take risks.

The sad reality about taking risks is that simply being true to yourself is rebellious these days. We have been so programmed to be what other people want us to be, that simply embracing your true authentic self is a courageous act. That's the only way to live this one life that you have. Once you get in tune with who you are, then it is time to do what it is that makes you happy. That is true freedom. Living the life that you orchestrated and designed. Living a life that correlates with your vision, values, character, energy, and overall being. What could be better than this?

I was reading this book entitled *Courage, the Joy of Living Dangerously*, by Osho and I came across a very deep, yet simple statement. He mentioned something along the lines of how people do not truly want to be happy because they have invested so much time into their misery. That is deep. When you analyze the world around you, you see this constantly. We cling to foods that we know are killing us. We cling to relationships that are unhealthy for us. We cling to distractions that are doing absolutely nothing for our growth. We cling to gossip; we cling to a lot of unproductive and destructive things.

If you are at a place in your life right now, where you are unhappy, then you KNOW that is time for something to change. Trust me, I am actually in this space as I write this book. That is the exact reason why I am writing this book, because it is what I would rather do with my life, so I need to put my all into it so it can be a source of my freedom. But back to YOU, if you are unhappy, then it is time to stop doing whatever it is that you are doing right now that is causing you to be unhappy. This is what being bold means.

Trust me, it's not worth it. You want to be unhappy, doing something you dread for 40 plus years, and then retire and try to cram in a ton of living in a matter of years? I recently was told that a person who had JUST retired died suddenly of a heart attack. That put things into perspective for me. I mean here was this guy who gave a job 40 plus years of his life and energy, and right when he thought he would be able to sit back and relax, he dies. This is just not the way to go through life. We deserve so much more. If you are going to devote all of your time and energy to something, why not devote it to something you actually care about?

It's time to take off that mask. It is time to stop being what everyone else thinks that you should be. It is time to stop living for everyone else, and to start living for yourself. This really should not have to be said, but most of us are not living the life that we should. You have to be fearless; you cannot worry about how you will be perceived by others once you decide to travel down this courageous path. You will be met with a lot of resistance, simply because people do not understand this lifestyle.

Anytime you begin to make positive changes in your life, people will treat you differently. Why? Well, the answer is simple, people envy what they wish they could accomplish at times. It's almost like a secret form of admiration, but they wrongly disguise this admiration with hatred, doubt, envy, and jealously. You know, when you start expressing your dreams/plans with someone and those plans involve you taking risks in life, or elevating your health they tell you how they don't think that the plans you have will workout well.

There are several ways you can deal with these types of mentalities. The first way to handle these people is by not sharing your dreams and plans with them. Instead, just let them witness the finished product; make them a believer that way. At the end of the day, you don't owe it to anyone to share your dreams with them. You are simply just being friendly and sociable when you do this, remember this, you don't have to share your plans with everybody and you shouldn't share them with any and everybody.

The second way to deal with dream killers is to neutralize their negativity with constant positivity. This technique is for the strong mind who is not bothered by the doubt, and instead sees it as an opportunity to further educate people around him/her on why they will succeed, or why the life they have chosen is the best life for them. You will notice once you become THAT person, people will stop bringing that doubtful energy your way when it comes to your lifestyle, because they don't want to receive another lecture from you. This is a sad case, because when it comes to things like eating healthy, taking risks to live the life you deserve, you would think more people would want to be motivated to do these things.

Don't let people discourage you from being original and fearless in this world. At first, it may be a lonely road, but once people see that you are dedicated to certain lifestyle shifts, they will begin to respect you more, and may even come to you with questions. It's not your job to live for other people. It's not your job to worry about offending people due to changes you feel you need to make. If you feel as if you need to move, or live a certain type of way, then DO JUST THAT, make the shift.

What is one of the more popular quotes when it comes to taking risks in life? You've heard this one before, several times, the bigger the risk the bigger the reward. This goes back to what I was saying about being bold. Just observe the direction that this world is headed in. We have robots taking essential jobs from humans. Plus, the jobs that even exist for most people currently don't pay enough to cover the basic necessities of life. This forces people to work several jobs, AND still lack enough funds to cover the essentials. Something has to be done. I know we are tired of giving all of our time to these corporations, neglecting our families and freedom. Time is of the essence, and it waits for no man, woman, or child.

I am big on the concept of controlling your time. That is true freedom. Being able to move when and how you want to move. Not being tied down to the rules and regulations of another system. The only way to achieve this level of freedom in my mind is by being bold and taking risks. If it seems crazy, then it may be the best option for you to take. If it's an idea that most people will frown upon, chances are it may be the idea that gets you to where you need to be in life.

You have to be a revolutionary, visionary, and rebel in regards to how you approach living your life these days. Honestly, if majority of the people agree to something, then I am typically the person who will take the opposing route. You have to be willing to go against the grain and become uncomfortable in order to grow. As a personal trainer this is the only way to consistently get the results that you desire. You have to increase the intensity of your workouts, by adding more weights, decreasing the rest time, doing more reps, or doing completely different exercises. The moral here is that you cannot allow your body to get comfortable with the same routine, or else it will stop growing and providing you with results.

Use this same approach to life. Constantly look for ways to increase your efforts and productivity. Challenge your BRAIN/MIND on a consistent basis. Your brain is a muscle, and just like a muscle, if you fail to exercise the brain muscle it will go to waste. You have to be willing to do what other people are not doing in order to attain the life you deserve. I challenge you to be a revolutionary. I challenge you to be bold and authentic. I challenge you to be great.

5. *BUILDING BETTER HABITS*

I touched on establishing better habits briefly when I discussed creating a morning routine. But in this section I will elaborate more on the importance of establishing better habits, and just exactly how to go about building them. You are the sum total of your habits, and you will only go as far as the habits you possess. For some of us this is a good thing, but for others this can be a challenge because over the years we have established very poor habits.

EMBRACE THE PROCESS, NOT THE ACTUAL GOAL

Listen, I understand how exciting it is to create a very big goal and how much time you want to spend visualizing the attainment of the goal. This can prove to be problematic though. What tends to happen to most people is that we get so lost in fantasizing about the end goal, that we forget to focus on the small, baby steps that it takes to actually get there. Sitting around visualizing yourself as a millionaire, won't do much for you if you fail to adopt the habits of a millionaire. I don't care how many affirmations you repeat, and how often you meditate on the goal, if you fail to put the proper system in play to achieve the goal, you will never reach it.

Let's look at sports for an example of what I mean here. Every team should have the same end goal in mind for the most part, and that is to win a championship. That is cool, but let me tell you this, how could a team win a championship if they neglected practice and failed to put the proper systems and strategies in play day in and day out? They would not get too far if they just focused on winning the championship. You hear it all the time when players talk about taking it one game at a time, and not looking to far ahead into the future, because that will cause them to overlook their opponents. You need to adopt this same mentality towards your goals. Don't overlook the seemingly small, yet necessary tasks required to get you to that big goal.

CREATING YOUR SYSTEM

When it comes to creating your system, this will be different from person to person because we all have different goals. One of the first things you need to do first though is establish just exactly what your major goal is first. What is it that you want to accomplish in the future? We tend to have a lot of goals, but I recommend minimizing the goals to start off here. Start off by focusing on maybe 2-3 major goals, something that may take you a few months or years to complete.

Once you have established what goals you are striving for, now it's time to analyze yourself and your daily habits.

The first thing you need to ask yourself is what habits do you currently have that will prevent you from reaching these goals? What habits do you possess that are holding you back currently? There are obviously some habits that you have that are holding you back, or else you would've already been in the position to reach your goals.

Once you have figured out what is hindering you, it is now time to find out just exactly what you need to do on a day-to-day, or weekly basis to accomplish the goals. What actions can you take daily and weekly on a consistent basis that will propel you towards your goals? Obviously here, these will be actions that you are either currently not taking, or you have been inconsistent with over the years.

Ok, now we know what we cannot do, and what we need to do in order to reach our goals. We are getting that much closer to creating our system. Next thing we need to focus on is just exactly how do we eliminate, or minimize these bad habits, and how do we build these better habits? It sounds as simple as simply stop doing what's bad, and start doing what we know we need to do, but it's really not that simple and if you look at it as such you will definitely fail.

HOW TO BREAK BAD HABITS

There is a book entitled *Atomic Habits* that has a lot of great information on how to break bad habits and build better ones. I will be using what I learned from that book in the next few sections along with my own implementations to give you a clear guide on how to deal with the art of breaking and building habits. In the book, the author gives you four laws on how to break bad habits.

LAW 1: MAKE IT INVISIBLE

The first law that the author suggests is to make the bad habit invisible. This revolves around removing cues of the bad habit from your environment, which reduces your exposure to the habit. Every bad habit that you have has a trigger. There is something that when you come across it, it influences you to partake in that bad habit, whatever that trigger, or cue is, you need to reduce your exposure to it, plain and simple.

In the book, the author talked about people who are disciplined, and the perception that most people have of these people. The main perception that people have of those who are considered disciplined is that they possess a lot of willpower and self-control. Well, in a sense that could be accurate, but it may not necessarily be the proper way to perceive what it means to be disciplined.

What if I told you that instead of focusing on using an immense amount of willpower and self-control, that people who are disciplined simply structure their lives in ways that requires them to use LESS willpower and self-control? Just think about it. It makes sense, because it is much easier to practice self-control when you don't have to use it as much. The problem that most of us have is that we place ourselves in tempting environments WAY TOO OFTEN that is just asking for the worse.

The key to making your bad habits invisible is simply reducing your exposure to the triggers. Change up your environment and surround yourself instead with triggers that will influence your good habits that you are trying to build. Don't focus on trying to use an enormous amount of willpower, or self-control. If you have a bad habit of eating candy, simply stop buying the candy and buy more fruits. Reduce your exposure, and create an environment that aligns more with your good habits.

MAKE IT UGLY (UNATTRACTIVE)

This one is quite simple and self-explanatory. When it comes to destroying bad habits, we have literally justified our bad habits/cravings by mentioning how good the habit may make us feel. For example, we have heard the countless times someone has said that eating that ice cream or candy makes them happy, or that it just tastes sooooo good that they can't imagine NOT eating it. We tend to embrace a delusional mentality when it comes to our bad habits.

Instead of striving to justify the irrational, it is time to face the music and focus on the benefits of avoiding your bad habits. Also, you can be more mindful of the dangers that are associated with the bad habits as well. This will cause you to be more cautious when you even consider going backwards and slipping up. Instill it in your mind right now. Focus on how beneficial it will be to avoid the habits that are holding you back right now.

If procrastination is a bad habit that you have and you are striving to break this habit, here is how you should perceive it. What will happen if you break this habit? You will be more productive, and you will get more work done. Why is this important? It will allow you to accomplish more of your goals in life, and can lead to an increase in income, health, and overall peace.

On the other hand, what happens if you continue to procrastinate? You continue to be unproductive and you don't get much work done. Why is this bad? You will continue to be stagnant, and this may even cause you to regress. This will eventually lead to a decline in your finances, health, and overall well-being. This should be common sense, but most of us rationalize our procrastination, by indulging in unproductive activities that we feel are more enjoyable than getting important things done.

Lastly, think about it this way. The more you get done NOW, the more you can sit back and do those activities that you may enjoy in the future. But, the more you procrastinate NOW, the less time you will have in the future to enjoy, and have control over your life. Make your bad habits unattractive by highlighting the positives that arise from avoiding the bad habits. Also, highlight the dangers that come with continuing to partake in the bad habits.

MAKE IT DIFFICULT

The third part of the process in regards to destroying a bad habit revolves around making the habit difficult to indulge in. This kind of ties into when I was talking about reducing exposure to the triggers that causes you to act on your bad habits. Here, we more so want to focus on reducing the friction. They say the greater the friction, the less likely the habit.

You may be wondering how in the world do you reduce the friction. Well, I'll go back to the procrastination example. Let's say that one of your problems with procrastination is that you are easily distracted. You are constantly checking your phone, browsing around, looking at any and everything other than what you need to be looking at and doing. We've all been there, our phones are probably one of the most counterproductive devices known to man at this point. They serve many purposes, but they do indeed cause us to become terribly distracted too often and too easy.

With that being said, we need to find a way to reduce the friction in regards to us being distracted by this phone, which is causing us to continually procrastinate. This one is simple, how about you keep your phone in another room while you handle your important business. Either leave it in another room, or simply turn it off when it's time to get work done. Don't worry, the phone will be there when you are done, you won't miss much.

Another great tactic in regards to our phones that I have found to be useful is deleting your social media apps for a brief period of time. Let's face it, too many of us are consumed by social media, and a lot of us would accomplish so much more in life, if we spent less time browsing these sites looking for entertainment. Try deleting your app for a week or so, or at least until you complete a major task. That could be like your reward for getting some important work done, you can go back to wasting time on social media because you've accomplished something of importance.

If you have bad eating habits and you want to change the way you eat, then this strategy is also beneficial. This too, goes hand-in-hand with creating a less tempting environment. If you have a problem with snacks, then you could either just stop buying the snacks, or if you buy them, buy less of them and then bury them deep into your freezers or pantries. Let's face it, we are lazy individuals, if it requires a lot of work we will tend to think twice about it. We are wired to take the path of least resistance. If that ice cream is buried all the way in the back of the freezer, then chances are you will think twice about going after the ice cream because it will take too much work!

MAKE IT UNSATISFYING

This is probably one of my favorite strategies right here. This pretty much involves punishing yourself for indulging in harmful habits. We do this, and see this done to children all of the time. Sadly, we can learn a lot from how we treat children in regards to how we treat ourselves. You even see this done with pets, mainly dogs a lot too. You punish that dog when it does something destructive.

Let me clear this up too. Punishment doesn't automatically equate to physical harm. When I was a child, and I failed to get decent grades in school, instead of a whooping, my mother would take my controllers to my video game from me. Or, I wouldn't be able to play basketball. Those restrictions hit a lot harder for me at that time than any whooping would've done. This forced me to focus on keeping my grades up and acting right in school, because I DID NOT want my mother to take away my video games and basketball.

You should see where I am going with this strategy by now. Whatever bad habit you have, it is time to start holding yourself accountable for slipping up. If you have to treat yourself like you treat your children, then so be it. Whatever it takes to get the job done is what we will do, because bad habits are destroying you, and slowing up your progress right now. Even if you have to get an accountability partner to keep you in check, then do that. Some of us need that external push to get us going in the right direction and keep us on that right path.

As a personal trainer, I am pretty much that accountability coach to my clients. Just think about it, clients have signed a contract, paying me money to guide them through a workout, something that they've KNOWN for years that they should've been doing. Now, I don't know about you all, but I don't like wasting money, so if I sign up for something, then I am going to make sure I am going to get my money's worth. What better way to punish yourself, than to lose money? Nobody likes losing money, NOBODY!

This leads me to talk about a great method that I came across in the *Atomic Habits* book. It revolves around finding that accountability partner. It can be an actual accountability coach, your spouse, mother, father, brother, sister, children, anyone. The trick is this; you need to sign a contract with that individual/individuals. I would prefer you include stipulations that involve your finances, because this will motivate you a lot more to make sure you are doing what needs to be done. Do this right now; think of someone that you can assign this role to. It has to be someone that will actually hold you accountable and stick to the terms of the contract.

Once you find this person, then it is time to discuss the terms of the contract. One great method as I said earlier revolves around a financial punishment for you slipping up. Let's say, you have this goal to lose 20 pounds in 3 months.

The healthy way to lose the weight is about a pound and a half to two pounds a week. Let's say you fail to lose any weight for the week, you have to pay your accountability partner $20 dollars for each week you fail to drop at least one pound.

I guarantee you that this will make you more determined to reach your goal, because NOBODY likes giving away money like that. This will force you to make the commitment to achieving the goal. Losing money is very unsatisfying. This is one of the best methods in regards to having an accountability partner that I suggest because it hits where it tends to hurt the most, the pockets.

We have discussed ways to eliminate or at least minimize the bad habits that we have. Well, if you simply just take the opposite of each approach I mentioned, then you will have the methods that are best used to establish better habits. Make it visible, make it attractive, make it easy, and make it satisfying. And you would just simply take the opposing approach, and then there you have it, you will be on the path to building and establishing better habits.

6. *REMAIN CALM*

Listen, when it comes to this life, you have to understand something very basic, you are not the only one going through rough times. What would life be without the so-called negative experiences? There would be no life without this duality; it is necessary to keep the world in proper order. You are a reflection of what goes on in this universe, because the universe is you, and you are the universe.

This is not some deep, esoteric knowledge. It's common sense, if you just sit back and observe. Just pay attention to nature. Nature is not 100% positive; a lot of destruction takes place within nature. We witness a lot of destructive storms via nature, and that makes us appreciate the days of pure sunshine that much more. Your life is a reflection of this.

There will be plenty of storms that come into your life, that hinder your light from shining. But, you have to understand that the storm is temporary, it is not a permanent occurrence. Learn to embrace that storm, take the best parts from it. You may have been experiencing a mental drought, and that storm is just what you needed for some seeds you planted to start growing and get you going back into the right direction.

What tends to happen is we like to just focus on the negatives or the storms that come into our lives. As my favorite saying goes, what you focus on grows. If you only focus on your struggles, then your struggles will continue to grow. Simply acknowledge the struggles, but shift your focus towards the lessons to be learned within the struggles and the solutions.

I am big on improving the quality of your mind and thoughts. Mental health is a problem with a lot of people in the WORLD. I know I've had my battles in the past, and I continue to have mental battles to this day, but I am learning how to deal with the issues. With the way the world is set up, many of us are stuck doing things that we may not enjoy, forcing us to be in environments that may not be conducive to our health and well being. How do we cope with such a situation, knowing we only have one life to live to get it right?

First things first, you cannot take the stressing out approach. When you stress yourself out consistently you are literally killing yourself and weakening your immune system. This is definitely not a helpful way to combat and alter your circumstances. You have to be strong in this sense, because you will have go back to what I said in previous chapters and be bold here. Your health & sanity are more important than a job, or corporation.

You have to plant positive seeds in your mind on a daily basis. Don't allow anything to alter this approach. You must also begin to eliminate the unnecessary chatter that goes on in your mind. This is where remaining calm comes into play. A lot of people practice meditation, and there are a TON of benefits that come with meditation. I would definitely recommend meditation as a method to reducing stress, and elevating your mental and physical health.

A lot of people have trouble initially when it comes to meditation. Telling someone to just sit down comfortably, be quiet, and don't focus on your thoughts is almost as challenging for some people if not more than suggesting they change up their eating habits. We tend to entertain too many thoughts on a daily basis, and most of the time we overthink and focus on a lot of unproductive and destructive thoughts. We stop the thoughts, instead of just letting them come and go, as they will naturally do. Instead, we tend to make big deals out of little thoughts.

The way I suggest that you start mediating is simply focusing on your breathing. This method helps me meditate better, because it gives me something to focus on, instead of just saying to not focus on my thoughts. Here, you just focus on your breathing. Be mindful of each breath that you take. That's it, it is that simple, take deep breaths, and just focus on each deep breath, intimately. Get relaxed and get comfortable then just breathe. You can start by just doing this for 5 minutes a day, and once you master this for 5 minutes then you can increase the duration of the exercise.

We have to start claiming our peace and sanity. We are too stressed as a society. Stress leads to dis-ease, weak immune systems, obesity, etc. You owe it to yourself to participate in practices that will alleviate your stress. Whether that is meditation, or just writing your thoughts down daily in a journal. Do what is necessary to manifest constant peace and positivity into your life. Overly stressing out will lead to self-destruction.

7. *The Marathon Continues*

If you are not familiar with the name Nipsey Hussle, don't worry I'll fill you in. He is most commonly known for being an emcee, or rapper. His music has touched the lives of many. He was born on the West Coast, raised in the Crenshaw area. I don't want to get into writing a biography about him, but I just wanted you to get his origins.

To me, and to plenty of others, Nipsey was more than a rapper. He was a visionary, he was an activist, he was an entrepreneur, and he was a great mind and role model. He represented for his community, and became a model of success. He was the living proof that no matter your circumstances you can come out on top as long as you stay committed, persistent, and dedicated to a positive purpose. He gave a lot of people in the inner cities hope. And he did not abandon the inner city; he frequently came back, and even opened up a store and employed people right there in the same area where he grew up. Sadly, that store is where he lost his physical life.

I learned a lot of valuable lessons from Nipsey, just by taking the words from his music, and analyzing some of his interviews. He was a constant source of motivation for me when I would be in the gym working out, or when I would need music to motivate me to get some work done. The energy and message in his music always inspired and continues to inspire me to always strive to elevate my game.

His last album was entitled, *Victory Lap*. This came after years of him making it known that the marathon continues. I want to focus on that concept of the marathon. I feel as if this is very valuable when it comes to you manifesting success in your life. I see too many people get discouraged out here when they don't get the results they want, quickly. We all want to get rich quick, lose weight fast, and build a successful business in days. We continue to ignore the art of patience. What is the saying? "Rome wasn't built in a day." Go find me any great empire or business that was built in a day, week, months, or even a year really. Greatness takes time, period. There will be a lot of ups and downs on your journey to this greatness but you have to embrace the art of patience and learn to be persistent.

Your word is your bond. If you cannot trust yourself to keep your own promises, then we have a serious issue on our hands. Life is life. It is not negative or positive, things will happen to you in life, and your perception is what creates the energy surrounding the things that occur. You have choices; you have power in this world. You can choose to remain stagnant, or you can choose to start building and manifesting that inner gold and greatness that exists within each and every one of us.

I am going to use a few lines from Nipsey in order to drive home some points before ending this book. One line he had was this, "I owe myself, I told myself back then that I would do this." There you go. Once you make a commitment to something, you owe it to yourself to at least follow through with it. In the beginning was the word; your word is all you have in the beginning. If you can't follow through on what you have said you would do then you will be in for an inconsistent, roller-coaster type of journey through life.

If you say you are going to lose 30 pounds. Then LOSE that 30 pounds. If you say you are going to double your income within the next 6 months, then DOUBLE YOUR INCOME within the next 6 months. If you had plans of becoming an entrepreneur. Then BECOME AN ENTREPRENEUR. You have one life to get it right and leave a legacy behind. Do not waste it. Follow through on your words. Your word is your bond. Fulfill the promises you have made to yourself.

"I know that I can't win em' all, but I can't keep losing." Take these words from Nipsey Hussle to heart. Simple, yet very profound and effective if internalized. That's part of the marathon mentality. You may not get all of the wins that you would like to have, but you will definitely get some wins in the process. You just have to keep executing and thinking the proper thoughts. Even within the losses, you will be able to learn about your weaknesses (self) during the process, and see where you need to improve, so that's not really a loss.

Life is truly a marathon. It's a long and slow grind. You have to pace yourself, and the worse thing you can do is try to run at the pace of someone else. That is a sure way to burn yourself out. Find your pace and stick to running YOUR race. And remember this, sometimes the victory isn't the fact that you finished before others; the victory could be as simple as you finishing the race! The marathon continues. Rest In Power to Nipsey Hussle, and let's all get started on our marathon in life, conquer these goals, and begin manifesting success in abundance. The world is yours, the world is you, you are powerful, and nothing but success and greatness awaits you!

www.ingramcontent.com/pod-product-compliance
Lightning Source LLC
Chambersburg PA
CBHW031216090426
42736CB00009B/939